Planet Explorers

Story by Phillip Simpson

Illustrations by Wendy Tan

Planet Explorers

Text: Phillip Simpson
Publishers: Tania Mazzeo and Eliza Webb
Series consultant: Amanda Sutera,
  Hands on Heads Consulting
Editor: Gemma Smith
Project editor: Annabel Smith
Designer: Jess Kelly
Project designer: Danielle Maccarone
Illustrations: Wendy Tan
Production controller: Renee Tome

NovaStar

Text © 2024 Cengage Learning Australia Pty Limited
Illustrations © 2024 Cengage Learning Australia Pty Limited

ISBN 978 0 17 033410 5

Cengage Learning Australia
Level 5, 80 Dorcas Street
Southbank VIC 3006 Australia
Phone: 1300 790 853
Email: aust.nelsonprimary@cengage.com

For learning solutions, visit **cengage.com.au**

Printed in China by 1010 Printing International Ltd
1 2 3 4 5 6 7 28 27 26 25 24

*Nelson acknowledges the Traditional Owners and Custodians
of the lands of all First Nations Peoples. We pay respect
to Elders past and present, and extend that respect to
all First Nations Peoples today.*

Contents

Chapter 1

A New Planet

"Let's go in!" shouted my brother, Leo, his eyes glowing with excitement.

"I don't know if we should," I said, looking nervously into the dark mouth of the cave. "Mum and Dad told us to stay away from anything dangerous."

"We have to go in, Zara," said Leo. "It's our duty as planet explorers. We need to make sure that every part of this planet is safe."

I knew Leo was right. I had to be brave. Earth was dying and humans needed to find a new planet to live on.

Leo adjusted his helmet slightly.
Our spacesuits were annoying, but
Mum and Dad had made us wear them.
Their tests had shown that the
atmosphere on this planet was breathable,
but they weren't taking any chances.

This was the first planet we had landed
on that looked anything like Earth.
There were clear blue skies, clean
sparkling lakes and oceans, and huge
green forests as far as the eye could see.

But Mum wanted us to be extra careful.
"Until we can do some more tests,
the suits and helmets stay on,"
she had said.

"And keep your communicators switched on,"
Dad had added.

After all, this was an unexplored planet.
We had no idea what surprises it had
in store for us.

Chapter 2

Searching the Galaxy

"It'll be fine, Zara," Leo was saying. "This cave looks just like the ones on Earth. Besides, Mum and Dad are only a call away."

I nodded slowly. I had to be more adventurous. After all, I was part of an adventurous family who had been chosen to explore the galaxy.

The Planet Exploration Board had asked for volunteers to search for new planets. Climate change had melted Earth's ice caps, causing the sea levels to rise and whole countries to disappear. Many people were left without anywhere to live, and there was less land for growing food.

That's why we urgently needed to find new planets. The Planet Exploration Board had even given each family who had agreed to explore the galaxy their own spaceship.

Mum and Dad were scientists, and Leo
and I wanted to be planet explorers.
So, of course we had volunteered!

Chapter 3

Into the Darkness

Leo led the way into the cave. I followed close behind him, turning on my helmet light. In front of me, Leo did the same. The beams of light stabbed out into the darkness, brightening the dark cave.
I looked around, amazed. The cave walls were a beautiful mix of rainbow colours that sparkled under our helmet lights.

But, as we moved deeper into the cave, our lights flashed on something else – something that moved in the shadows.

"Did you see that?" I asked my brother.

Leo nodded.

"I think we should go back to the spaceship," I said.

"In a minute," said Leo. "Let's find out what it is first. Remember, we're planet explorers!"

I felt uneasy, but I followed Leo into the darkness anyway. He was right. What sort of explorer would I be if I wasn't prepared to investigate?

We moved forward, the lights on our helmets shining on the far wall. Suddenly, we found what was moving ...

There, at the back of the cave, were hundreds of creatures bobbing about. They looked a bit like floating octopuses, with round heads, staring black eyes and lots of tentacles that waved around in the air. Each creature was a different colour of the rainbow.

The creatures must have been attracted to our lights, because suddenly, they started coming towards us.

"Aliens!" shouted Leo, his voice high and nervous, as he turned back towards the cave entrance. "Let's get out of here!"

Chapter 4

An Alien Encounter

Something strange happened then. Something hard to describe. One of the creatures landed gently on my arm. As it did so, I suddenly had a feeling that these creatures meant us no harm. Instead of being scared like my brother, I felt calm.

Leo was already close to the cave entrance. He turned back towards me. "Come on, Zara!" he shouted. "We need to leave!"

I ignored him. More of the creatures were coming even closer – hundreds of them floating towards me. Their beautiful colourful bodies sparkled in the light from my helmet.

"It's okay," I said. "I don't think they want to hurt us."

"Watch out!" called Leo.

I turned just as more of the creatures reached me. I suddenly felt a little nervous. Not scared, just a little unsure. This was humankind's first encounter with an alien species, after all. What did they want?

And then I knew. Somehow, just by touching my suit with their tentacles, the alien creatures were communicating with me.

"Welcome," said a voice inside my head. "We look forward to sharing our way of life with you, and showing you how we care for our planet." I could hear the creatures' voices in my head, without them speaking!

I closed my eyes. In my mind, I said, "Thank you," mostly because I didn't know what else to say. What do you say to the first aliens you've ever met?

Chapter 5

New Friends

More of the creatures came to land on me, until most of my spacesuit was covered with the little brightly coloured aliens.

Leo must have returned from the cave's entrance, because suddenly he was at my side. He looked worried.

"Are you okay?" he asked.

I nodded. Not only had the creatures welcomed me, but they had made me feel safe and happy. Somehow, I knew that humans and these creatures could live together and help each other.

"Couldn't be better," I said, smiling at my brother. Then, several of the little creatures dropped onto Leo's suit, touching him with their tentacles.

At first, he looked scared, but then his face broke into a huge smile as the creatures started communicating with him, too.

"Let's go back to the spaceship and tell Mum and Dad what we've discovered!" I said.

Leo's smile grew even wider, and he nodded. "I'm proud of you, Zara," he said. "Wait until Mum and Dad hear what a great explorer you've become!"

This planet, I knew, was going to work out just fine.